W9-BEM-415

WOMEN/MEN EDITION
VOLUME 12

HAL•LEONARD

ro vocal®
BETTER THAN KARAOKE!

Frozen

SING 7 SONGS WITH SOUND-ALIKE AUDIO TRACKS

To access audio visit:
www.halleonard.com/mylibrary

Enter Code
7618-5587-8985-7747

ISBN 978-1-4803-8642-6

WONDERLAND MUSIC COMPANY, INC.

DISTRIBUTED BY

HAL•LEONARD®
CORPORATION

7777 W. BLUEMOUND RD. P.O. BOX 13819 MILWAUKEE, WI 53213

Disney characters and artwork © Disney Enterprises, Inc.

In Australia Contact:
Hal Leonard Australia Pty. Ltd.
4 Lentara Court
Cheltenham, Victoria, 3192 Australia
Email: ausadmin@halleonard.com.au

Visit Hal Leonard Online at
www.halleonard.com

Do You Want to Build a Snowman?

Music and Lyrics by Kristen Anderson-Lopez and Robert Lopez

snow - man? It does-n't have to be a

snow - man. *(Spoken:)* Go away, Anna.

LITTLE ELSA:

LITTLE ANNA:

(Sung:) O - kay, bye.

(knocking)

YOUNG ANNA: Do you want to build a snow - man? Or ride our bikes a-round the

halls? I think some com-pan-y is o-ver-due; I've start-ed

talk-ing to the pic-tures on the walls. *(Spoken:) Hang in there, Joan!* *(Sung:)* It gets a lit-tle

lone - ly, all these emp-ty ___ rooms, ___ just watch-ing the hours tick

by. *(click tongue)*

3

Interlude

36

N.C.

A little slower, tenderly

(knocking)   **ANNA:** *(Spoken:)* Elsa?   *(Sung:)* Please,   I   know you're

E♭sus2

3

B♭sus2/D

in there.   Peo - ple are ask - ing where you've been.

A♭/C

They   say, "Have cour - age,"   and I'm   try - ing   to;   I'm   right   out

Cm

Gm   G(sus2/4)   Gm

here for you,   just let me   in.   We on - ly have each

A♭

B♭/D   E♭

Dm7♭5   Ddim7

3

oth - er;   it's just   you   and   me. __   What   are   we   gon - na

C(sus2/4)   Cm   Cm7   Cm9

F7

do? _____

Slower

N.C.   E♭/G

9

Do   you   want   to   build   a   snow - man?

4

Fixer Upper

Music and Lyrics by Kristen Anderson-Lopez and Robert Lopez

With comic bounce

BULDA: *(Spoken:)* What's the issue, dear?
Why are you holding back from such a man?

(Sung:) Is it the clump-y way _ he walks? Or the grump-y way _ he talks? Or the pear-shaped, square-shaped weird-ness of his feet?

CLIFF:

FEMALE TROLL 1:

MALE TROLL 1: And though we know he wash-es well, _ he al-ways ends up sort-a smell-y.

BULDA: But you'll nev-er meet a fel-la who's as sen-si-tive _ and sweet!

BULDA & CLIFF: So he's a bit of a fix-er up-per; so he's got _ a few flaws, like his pe-

FEMALE TROLL 2:

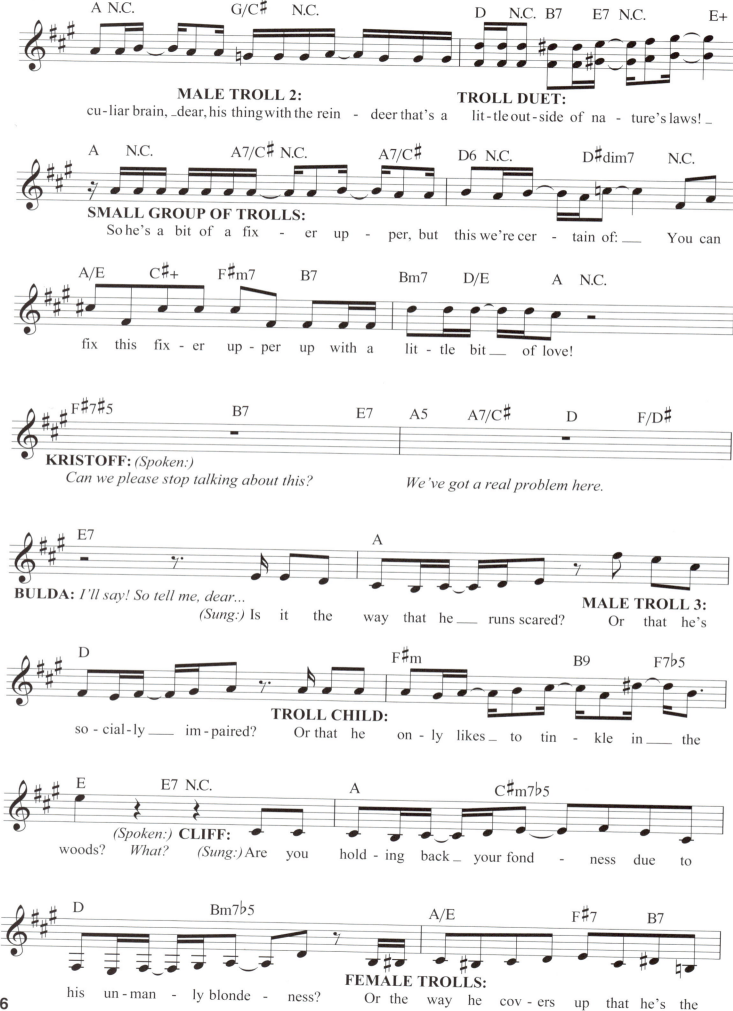

MALE TROLL 2:
cu-liar brain, _dear, his thing with the rein - deer that's a   lit-tle out-side of na - ture's laws! _

TROLL DUET:

SMALL GROUP OF TROLLS:
So he's a bit of a fix - er up - per, but this we're cer - tain of: ___   You can

fix this fix - er up - per up with a   lit - tle bit ___ of love!

KRISTOFF: *(Spoken:)*
Can we please stop talking about this?   *We've got a real problem here.*

BULDA: *I'll say! So tell me, dear...*
          (Sung:) Is it the   way that he ___ runs scared?   Or that he's

MALE TROLL 3:

TROLL CHILD:
so - cial-ly ___ im - paired?   Or that he   on - ly likes _ to tin - kle in ___ the

(Spoken:) **CLIFF:**
woods?   *What?*   *(Sung:)* Are you   hold - ing back _ your fond - ness due to

FEMALE TROLLS:
his un - man - ly blonde - ness?   Or the   way he cov - ers up that he's the

hon - est ___ goods? **ALL TROLLS:** He's just a bit of a fix - er up - per;

he's got a cou-ple-a bugs. _ His i - so - la - tion is con - fir - ma - tion of his

des-per-a - tion for heal-ing hugs! _ So he's a bit of a fix - er up - per, but

we know what _ to do: ___ the way to fix up this fix - er up - per is to

fix him up ___ with you! **KRISTOFF:** *(Spoken:)* ENOUGH!

She is engaged to someone else, okay?

CLIFF:
(Sung:) So she's a bit of a fix - er up - per; that's a mi - nor thing. _ **MALE TROLL 4:** **MALE TROLL 5:** Her

quote "en - gage - ment" is a flex ar - range - ment. And **TROLL CHILD:** by the way, I don't see ___ no ring!

7

MALE TROLLS: So she's a bit of a fix - er up - per; her brain's a bit __ be - twixt! __ Get the

fi - an - cé __ out of the way __ and the whole thing will __ be fixed!

Soulfully

BULDA: We're not say - ing you can change him, __ 'cause peo - ple don't real - ly change. __ We're

on - ly say - ing that love's __ a force __ that's pow er - ful __ and strange. __

Peo - ple make __ bad choic - es if they're mad or scared __ or stressed. __ But

throw a lit - tle love __ their way, _____ and

FEMALE TROLLS: (Throw a lit - tle love __ their way,

ALL TROLLS:
you'll bring out __ their best! True love brings out __ the best! _____
you'll bring out __ their best!) _

Ev - 'ry - one's a bit of a fix - er up - per; that's what it's all __ a - bout! CLIFF: Fa - ther!

For the First Time in Forever

Music and Lyrics by Kristen Anderson-Lopez and Robert Lopez

ANNA: The win-dow is o - pen! So's that door! I did-n't know they did that an - y - more. Who knew we owned eight thou - sand sal - ad plates? For years I've roamed these emp - ty halls. Why have a ball - room with no balls? Fi - nal-ly, they're o - p'ning up the gates! There'll be ac - tual real live peo - ple; it-'ll be to - tal-ly, strange. But, wow! Am I so read - y for this

Expressively

C(sus2/4) — F/A — B♭(add2)

change! 'Cause for the first time in for - ev - er, there'll be

C/E — F(add2) — F/E — Dm

mu - sic, there'll _ be light. ___ For the first time in for - ev -

Am — E♭ — A7

- er, I'll be danc - ing through _ the night. ___ Don't

Dm — Dm/C — B♭maj7

know if I'm e - lat - ed or gas - sy, but I'm some-where in ___ that

G9/B — Fm/A♭ — B♭sus2

zone. 'Cause for the first time in for - ev - er, _____

Excited again

C7sus — Fsus — F — Fsus — F

(Spoken:) *(gasp:)*

I won't be ___ a - lone. ___ *I can't wait to meet everyone.* *What if I meet...*

Fsus — F — G♭ — C♭/G♭

THE one? *(Sung:)* To - night, i - mag - ine me, gown _ and all, _

G♭maj7 — C♭/G♭ — G♭ — G♭/B♭

fetch - ing - ly draped _ a - gainst _ the wall, _ the pic - ture of ___ so - phis - ti - cat - ed

dream I'd find __ ro - mance, but for the first time in for - ev -

- er, _____ at least __ I've got __ a chance. __

ELSA: Don't let them in, don't let them __ see.

Be the good girl __ you al-ways have to be. __ Con - ceal,

don't feel, put on a show. Make one wrong move, and ev -'ry-one will

know. But it's on-ly for to - day! **ANNA:** It's on-ly for to - day! It's ag - o - ny to

wait! It's ag - o - ny to wait! Tell the guards to o - pen up the

In Summer

Music and Lyrics by Kristen Anderson-Lopez and Robert Lopez

Let It Go

Music and Lyrics by Kristen Anderson-Lopez and Robert Lopez

Half-time feel, mysterious

The snow glows white on the moun-tain to-night, _ not a foot-print _ to be seen. _ A king-dom of i - so-la -tion, and it looks like I'm the queen. _ The wind _ is howl - ing like _ this swirl - ing storm _ in - side. _ Could-n't keep it in, _ heav-en knows I _ tried. _

Don't let ___ them in, ___ don't let ___ them see. Be the good girl you

al-ways have ___ to be. Con-ceal, ___ don't feel, don't let ___ them know... ___

___ Well, now ___ they know. ___

___ Let it go, ___ let it go; ___ can't ___

hold it back an-y-more. ___ Let it go, ___ let it go; ___

___ turn a-way ___ and slam ___ the ___ door. ___

I ___ don't ___ care ___ what they're going to ___ say; ___

___ let the storm rage ___ on. ___ The

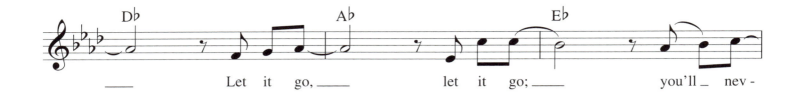

Let it go, ___ let it go; ___ you'll ___ nev-

-er see ___ me ___ cry. ___ Here ___ I ___ stand, ___

___ and here I'll ___ stay; _____ let the

storm rage ___ on. _____

My pow - er flur - ries through ___ the air ___ in - to ___ the ground. ___

My soul ___ is spi - ral - ing ___ in fro-

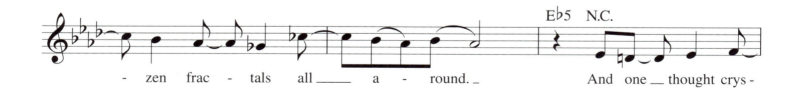

-zen frac - tals all _____ a - round. ___ And one ___ thought crys-

-tal - liz - es like ___ an ic - y blast: ___

I'm nev - er go - ing back; _ the past is in _ the past! _

_____ Let it go, _____ let it go, _

_ and I'll rise _ like the break _ of dawn. _ Let it go, _

_ let it go; _ that per - fect girl _ is _

gone. _____ Here _ I _ stand _ in the

light _ of _ day; _____ let the

storm rage _ on. _____ The

cold nev - er both - ered me an - y - way.

Love Is an Open Door

Music and Lyrics by Kristen Anderson-Lopez and Robert Lopez

Reindeer(s) Are Better Than People

Music and Lyrics by Kristen Anderson-Lopez and Robert Lopez

KRISTOFF: Rein - deers are better than peo - ple. Sven, don't you think that's true? **KRISTOFF (as Sven):** Yeah, peo - ple will beat you and curse you and cheat you. Ev - 'ry one of 'em's bad, ex - cept you. **KRISTOFF:** *(Spoken:) Aw, thanks buddy!*

Pro Vocal® Series

SONGBOOK & SOUND-ALIKE CD
SING GREAT SONGS WITH A PROFESSIONAL BAND

Whether you're a karaoke singer or an auditioning professional, the Pro Vocal® series is for you! Unlike most karaoke packs, each book in the Pro Vocal Series contains the lyrics, melody, and chord symbols for at least eight hit songs. The CD contains demos for listening, and separate backing tracks so you can sing along. The CD is playable on any CD player, but it is also enhanced so PC and Mac computer users can adjust the recording to any pitch without changing the tempo! Perfect for home rehearsal, parties, auditions, corporate events, and gigs without a backup band.

WOMEN'S EDITIONS

00740247	**1. Broadway Songs**	$14.95
00740249	**2. Jazz Standards**	$15.99
00740246	**3. Contemporary Hits**	$14.95
00740277	**4. '80s Gold**	$12.95
00740299	**5. Christmas Standards**	$15.95
00740281	**6. Disco Fever**	$12.95
00740279	**7. R&B Super Hits**	$12.95
00740309	**8. Wedding Gems**	$12.95
00740409	**9. Broadway Standards**	$14.95
00740348	**10. Andrew Lloyd Webber**	$14.95
00740344	**11. Disney's Best**	$15.99
00740378	**12. Ella Fitzgerald**	$14.95
00740350	**14. Musicals of Boublil & Schönberg**	$14.95
00740377	**15. Kelly Clarkson**	$14.95
00740342	**16. Disney Favorites**	$15.99
00740353	**17. Jazz Ballads**	$14.99
00740376	**18. Jazz Vocal Standards**	$17.99
00740375	**20. Hannah Montana**	$16.95
00740354	**21. Jazz Favorites**	$14.99
00740374	**22. Patsy Cline**	$14.95
00740369	**23. Grease**	$14.95
00740367	**25. Mamma Mia**	$15.99
00740365	**26. Movie Songs**	$14.95
00740360	**28. High School Musical 1 & 2**	$14.95
00740363	**29. Torch Songs**	$14.95
00740379	**30. Hairspray**	$15.99
00740380	**31. Top Hits**	$14.95
00740384	**32. Hits of the '70s**	$14.95
00740388	**33. Billie Holiday**	$14.95
00740389	**34. The Sound of Music**	$16.99
00740390	**35. Contemporary Christian**	$14.95
00740392	**36. Wicked**	$17.99
00740393	**37. More Hannah Montana**	$14.95
00740396	**39. Christmas Hits**	$15.95
00740410	**40. Broadway Classics**	$14.95
00740415	**41. Broadway Favorites**	$14.99
00740416	**42. Great Standards You Can Sing**	$14.99
00740417	**43. Singable Standards**	$14.99
00740418	**44. Favorite Standards**	$14.99
00740419	**45. Sing Broadway**	$14.99
00740420	**46. More Standards**	$14.99
00740421	**47. Timeless Hits**	$14.99
00740422	**48. Easygoing R&B**	$14.99
00740424	**49. Taylor Swift**	$16.99
00740425	**50. From This Moment On**	$14.99
00740426	**51. Great Standards Collection**	$19.99
00740430	**52. Worship Favorites**	$14.99
00740434	**53. Lullabyes**	$14.99
00740438	**54. Lady Gaga**	$14.99
00740444	**55. Amy Winehouse**	$15.99
00740445	**56. Adele**	$16.99
00740446	**57. The Grammy Awards Best Female Pop Vocal Performance 1990-1999**	$14.99
00740447	**58. The Grammy Awards Best Female Pop Vocal Performance 2000-2009**	$14.99
00109374	**60. Katy Perry**	$14.99
00116334	**61. Taylor Swift Hits**	$14.99
00123120	**62. Top Downloads**	$14.99

MEN'S EDITIONS

00740250	**2. Jazz Standards**	$14.95
00740278	**4. '80s Gold**	$12.95
00740298	**5. Christmas Standards**	$15.95
00740280	**6. R&B Super Hits**	$12.95
00740282	**7. Disco Fever**	$12.95
00740310	**8. Wedding Gems**	$12.95
00740411	**9. Broadway Greats**	$14.99
00740333	**10. Elvis Presley – Volume 1**	$14.95
00740349	**11. Andrew Lloyd Webber**	$14.99
00740345	**12. Disney's Best**	$14.95
00740347	**13. Frank Sinatra Classics**	$14.95
00740334	**14. Lennon & McCartney**	$14.99
00740453	**15. Queen**	$14.99
00740335	**16. Elvis Presley – Volume 2**	$14.99
00740343	**17. Disney Favorites**	$14.99
00740351	**18. Musicals of Boublil & Schönberg**	$14.95
00740337	**19. Lennon & McCartney – Volume 2**	$14.99
00740346	**20. Frank Sinatra Standards**	$14.95
00740338	**21. Lennon & McCartney – Volume 3**	$14.99
00740358	**22. Great Standards**	$14.99
00740336	**23. Elvis Presley**	$14.99
00740341	**24. Duke Ellington**	$14.99
00740339	**25. Lennon & McCartney – Volume 4**	$14.99
00740359	**26. Pop Standards**	$14.99
00740362	**27. Michael Bublé**	$15.99
00740454	**28. Maroon 5**	$14.99
00740364	**29. Torch Songs**	$14.95
00740366	**30. Movie Songs**	$14.95
00740368	**31. Hip Hop Hits**	$14.95
00740370	**32. Grease**	$14.95
00740371	**33. Josh Groban**	$14.95
00740373	**34. Billy Joel**	$14.99
00740381	**35. Hits of the '50s**	$14.95
00740382	**36. Hits of the '60s**	$14.95
00740383	**37. Hits of the '70s**	$14.95
00740385	**38. Motown**	$14.95
00740386	**39. Hank Williams**	$14.95
00740387	**40. Neil Diamond**	$14.95
00740391	**41. Contemporary Christian**	$14.95
00740397	**42. Christmas Hits**	$15.95
00740399	**43. Ray**	$14.95
00740400	**44. The Rat Pack Hits**	$14.99
00740401	**45. Songs in the Style of Nat "King" Cole**	$14.99
00740402	**46. At the Lounge**	$14.95
00740403	**47. The Big Band Singer**	$14.95
00740404	**48. Jazz Cabaret Songs**	$14.99
00740405	**49. Cabaret Songs**	$14.99
00740406	**50. Big Band Standards**	$14.99
00740412	**51. Broadway's Best**	$14.99
00740427	**52. Great Standards Collection**	$19.99
00740431	**53. Worship Favorites**	$14.99
00740435	**54. Barry Manilow**	$14.99
00740436	**55. Lionel Richie**	$14.99
00740439	**56. Michael Bublé – Crazy Love**	$15.99
00740441	**57. Johnny Cash**	$14.99
00740442	**58. Bruno Mars**	$14.99
00740448	**59. The Grammy Awards Best Male Pop Vocal Performance 1990-1999**	$14.99
00740449	**60. The Grammy Awards Best Male Pop Vocal Performance 2000-2009**	$14.99
00740452	**61. Michael Bublé – Call Me Irresponsible**	$14.99

00101777	**62. Michael Bublé – Christmas**	$19.99
00102658	**63. Michael Jackson**	$14.99
00109288	**64. Justin Bieber**	$14.99

WARM-UPS

00740395	**Vocal Warm-Ups**	$14.99

MIXED EDITIONS

These editions feature songs for both male and female voices.

00740311	**1. Wedding Duets**	$12.95
00740398	**2. Enchanted**	$14.95
00740407	**3. Rent**	$14.95
00740408	**4. Broadway Favorites**	$14.99
00740413	**5. South Pacific**	$15.99
00740414	**6. High School Musical 3**	$14.99
00740429	**7. Christmas Carols**	$14.99
00740437	**8. Glee**	$16.99
00740440	**9. More Songs from Glee**	$21.99
00740443	**10. Even More Songs from Glee**	$15.99
00116960	**11. Les Misérables**	$19.99

KIDS EDITIONS

00740451	**1. Songs Children Can Sing!**	$14.99

Visit Hal Leonard online at
www.halleonard.com

7777 W. BLUEMOUND RD. P.O. BOX 13819 MILWAUKEE, WI 53213

Prices, contents, & availability subject to change without notice.

ORIGINAL KEYS FOR SINGERS

ACROSS THE UNIVERSE
Because • Blackbird • Hey Jude • Let It Be • Revolution • Something • and more.
00307010 Vocal Transcriptions with Piano $19.95

LOUIS ARMSTRONG
Dream a Little Dream of Me • Hello, Dolly! • Mack the Knife • Makin' Whoopee! • Mame • St. Louis Blues • What a Wonderful World • Zip-A-Dee-Doo-Dah • and more.
00307029 Vocal Transcriptions with Piano $19.99

THE BEATLES
And I Love Her • Blackbird • The Fool on the Hill • Here, There and Everywhere • I Will • Let It Be • Michelle • Something • With a Little Help from My Friends • and more.
00307400 Vocal Transcriptions with Piano $19.99

BROADWAY HITS (FEMALE SINGERS)
23 Broadway favorites from their most memorable renditions, including: And I Am Telling You I'm Not Going (Jennifer Hudson) • Cabaret (Liza Minelli) • Defying Gravity (Idina Menzel) • Edelweiss (Julie Andrews) • and more.
00119085 Vocal Transcriptions with Piano $19.99

BROADWAY HITS (MALE SINGERS)
23 timeless Broadway hits true to the men who made them famous: Bring Him Home (David Campbell) • If Ever I Would Leave You (Robert Goulet) • Oh, What a Beautiful Mornin' (Gordon MacRae) • and more.
00119084 Vocal Transcriptions with Piano $19.99

MARIAH CAREY
Always Be My Baby • Dreamlover • Emotions • Heartbreaker • Hero • I Don't Wanna Cry • Love Takes Time • Loverboy • One Sweet Day • Vision of Love • We Belong Together • and more.
00306835 Vocal Transcriptions with Piano $19.95

PATSY CLINE
Always • Blue Moon of Kentucky • Crazy • Faded Love • I Fall to Pieces • Just a Closer Walk with Thee • Sweet Dreams • more. Also includes a biography.
00740072 Vocal Transcriptions with Piano $16.99

ELLA FITZGERALD
A-tisket, A-tasket • But Not for Me • Easy to Love • Embraceable You • The Lady Is a Tramp • Misty • Oh, Lady Be Good! • Satin Doll • Stompin' at the Savoy • Take the "A" Train • and more. Includes a biography and discography.
00740252 Vocal Transcriptions with Piano $16.95

JOSH GROBAN
Alejate • Awake • Believe • February Song • In Her Eyes • Now or Never • O Holy Night • Per Te • The Prayer • To Where You Are • Un Amore Per Sempre • Un Dia Llegara • You Are Loved (Don't Give Up) • You Raise Me Up • You're Still You • and more.
00306969 Vocal Transcriptions with Piano $19.99

GREAT FEMALE SINGERS
Cry Me a River (Ella Fitzgerald) • Crazy (Patsy Cline) • Fever (Peggy Lee) • How Deep Is the Ocean (How High Is the Sky) (Billie Holiday) • Little Girl Blue (Nina Simone) • Tenderly (Rosemary Clooney) • and more.
00307132 Vocal Transcriptions with Piano $19.99

GREAT MALE SINGERS
Can't Help Falling in Love (Elvis Presley) • Georgia on My Mind (Ray Charles) • I've Got the World on a String (Frank Sinatra) • Mona Lisa (Nat King Cole) • Ol' Man River (Paul Robeson) • What a Wonderful World (Louis Armstrong) • and more.
00307133 Vocal Transcriptions with Piano $19.99

BILLIE HOLIDAY
TRANSCRIBED FROM HISTORIC RECORDINGS
Billie's Blues (I Love My Man) • Body and Soul • Crazy He Calls Me • Easy Living • A Fine Romance • God Bless' the Child • Lover, Come Back to Me • Miss Brown to You • Strange Fruit • The Very Thought of You • and more.
00740140 Vocal Transcriptions with Piano $17.99

JAZZ DIVAS
A collection of 30 ballads recorded by Ella Fitzgerald, Billie Holiday, Diana Krall, Nina Simone, Sarah Vaughan, and more! Includes: Black Coffee • It Might as Well Be Spring • The Man I Love • My Funny Valentine • and more.
00114959 Vocal Transcriptions with Piano $19.99

LADIES OF CHRISTMAS
Grown-Up Christmas List (Amy Grant) • Hard Candy Christmas (Dolly Parton) • Merry Christmas, Darling (Karen Carpenter) • Rockin' Around the Christmas Tree (Brenda Lee) • Santa Baby (Eartha Kitt) • and more.
00312192 Vocal Transcriptions with Piano $19.99

NANCY LAMOTT
Autumn Leaves • Downtown • I Have Dreamed • It Might as Well Be Spring • Moon River • Skylark • That Old Black Magic • and more.
00306995 Vocal Transcriptions with Piano $19.99

LEONA LEWIS – SPIRIT
Better in Time • Bleeding Love • The First Time Ever I Saw Your Face • Here I Am • Homeless • I Will Be • I'm You • Whatever It Takes • Yesterday • and more.
00307007 Vocal Transcriptions with Piano $17.95

CHRIS MANN
Always on My Mind • Ave Maria • Cuore • Falling • Longer • My Way • Need You Now • On a Night like This • Roads • Unless You Mean It • Viva La Vida.
00118921 Vocal Transcriptions with Piano $16.99

MEN OF CHRISTMAS
The Christmas Song (Chestnuts Roasting on an Open Fire) (Nat King Cole) • A Holly Jolly Christmas (Burl Ives) • It's Beginning to Look like Christmas (Perry Como) • White Christmas (Bing Crosby) • and more.
00312241 Vocal Transcriptions with Piano $19.99

THE BETTE MIDLER SONGBOOK
Boogie Woogie Bugle Boy • Friends • From a Distance • The Glory of Love • The Rose • Some People's Lives • Stay with Me • Stuff like That There • Ukulele Lady • The Wind Beneath My Wings • and more, plus a fantastic bio and photos.
00307067 Vocal Transcriptions with Piano $19.99

THE BEST OF LIZA MINNELLI
And All That Jazz • Cabaret • Losing My Mind • Maybe This Time • Me and My Baby • Theme from "New York, New York" • Ring Them Bells • Sara Lee • Say Liza (Liza with a Z) • Shine It On • Sing Happy • The Singer • Taking a Chance on Love.
00306928 Vocal Transcriptions with Piano $19.99

ONCE
All the Way Down • Broken Hearted Hoover Fixer Sucker Guy • Fallen from the Sky • Falling Slowly • Gold • The Hill • If You Want Me • Leave • Lies • Once • Say It to Me Now • Trying to Pull Myself Away • When Your Mind's Made Up.
00102569 Vocal Transcriptions with Piano $16.99

FRANK SINATRA – MORE OF HIS BEST
Almost like Being in Love • Cheek to Cheek • Fly Me to the Moon • I Could Write a Book • It Might as Well Be Spring • Luck Be a Lady • Old Devil Moon • Somebody Loves Me • When the World Was Young • and more.
00307081 Vocal Transcriptions with Piano $19.99

THE VERY BEST OF FRANK SINATRA
Come Fly with Me • I've Got You Under My Skin • It Was a Very Good Year • My Way • Night and Day • Summer Wind • The Way You Look Tonight • You Make Me Feel So Young • and more. Includes biography.
00306753 Vocal Transcriptions with Piano $19.95

STEVE TYRELL – BACK TO BACHARACH
Alfie • Always Something There to Remind Me • Close to You • I Say a Little Prayer • The Look of Love • Raindrops Keep Fallin' on My Head • This Guy's in Love with You • Walk on By • and more.
00307024 Vocal Transcriptions with Piano $16.99

THE BEST OF STEVE TYRELL
Ain't Misbehavin' • I Concentrate on You • I've Got a Crush on You • Isn't It Romantic? • A Kiss to Build a Dream On • Stardust • You'd Be So Nice to Come Home To • and more.
00307027 Vocal Transcriptions with Piano $16.99

SARAH VAUGHAN
Black Coffee • If You Could See Me Now • It Might as Well Be Spring • My Funny Valentine • The Nearness of You • A Night in Tunisia • Perdido • September Song • Tenderly • and more.
00306558 Vocal Transcriptions with Piano $17.95

VOCAL POP
Bad Romance • Bleeding Love • Breathe • Don't Know Why • Halo • I Will Always Love You • If I Ain't Got You • Rehab • Rolling in the Deep • Teenage Dream • You Belong with Me • and more!
00312656 Vocal Transcriptions with Piano $19.99

ANDY WILLIAMS – CHRISTMAS COLLECTION
Blue Christmas • Do You Hear What I Hear • Happy Holiday • The Little Drummer Boy • O Holy Night • Sleigh Ride • What Are You Doing New Year's Eve? • and more. Includes a great bio!
00307158 Vocal Transcriptions with Piano $17.99

ANDY WILLIAMS
Can't Get Used to Losing You • The Days of Wine and Roses • The Hawaiian Wedding Song (Ke Kali Nei Au) • The Impossible Dream • Moon River • More • The Most Wonderful Time of the Year • Red Roses for a Blue Lady • Speak Softly, Love • A Time for Us • Where Do I Begin • and more.
00307160 Vocal Transcriptions with Piano $17.99

HAL•LEONARD® CORPORATION
7777 W. BLUEMOUND RD. P.O. BOX 13819 MILWAUKEE, WI 53213

www.halleonard.com
Prices, contents, and availability subject to change without notice.

1113

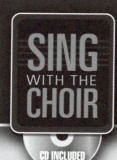

SING WITH THE CHOIR

CD INCLUDED

These **GREAT COLLECTIONS** let singers **BECOME PART OF A FULL CHOIR** and sing along with some of the most-loved songs of all time.

Each book includes SATB parts (arrangements are enlarged from octavo-size to 9" x 12") and the accompanying CD features full, professionally recorded performances.

Now you just need to turn on the CD, open the book, pick your part, and **SING ALONG WITH THE CHOIR!**

1. ANDREW LLOYD WEBBER
Any Dream Will Do • As If We Never Said Goodbye • Don't Cry for Me Argentina • Love Changes Everything • Memory • The Music of the Night • Pie Jesu • Whistle down the Wind.
00333001 Book/CD Pack $14.95

2. BROADWAY
Bring Him Home • Cabaret • For Good • Luck Be a Lady • Seasons of Love • There's No Business like Show Business • Where Is Love? • You'll Never Walk Alone.
00333002 Book/CD Pack $14.95

3. STANDARDS
Cheek to Cheek • Georgia on My Mind • I Left My Heart in San Francisco • I'm Beginning to See the Light • Moon River • On the Sunny Side of the Street • Skylark • When I Fall in Love.
00333003 Book/CD Pack $14.95

4. THE 1950s
At the Hop • The Great Pretender • Kansas City • La Bamba • Love Me Tender • My Prayer • Rock Around the Clock • Unchained Melody.
00333004 Book/CD Pack.............................. $14.95

5. THE 1960s
All You Need is Love • Can't Help Falling in Love • Dancing in the Street • Good Vibrations • I Heard It Through the Grapevine • I'm a Believer • Under the Boardwalk • What a Wonderful World.
00333005 Book/CD Pack.............................. $14.95

6. THE 1970s
Ain't No Mountain High Enough • Bohemian Rhapsody • I'll Be There • Imagine • Let It Be • Night Fever • Yesterday Once More • You Are the Sunshine of My Life.
00333006 Book/CD Pack.............................. $14.95

7. DISNEY FAVORITES
The Bare Necessities • Be Our Guest • Circle of Life • Cruella De Vil • Friend like Me • Hakuna Matata • Joyful, Joyful • Under the Sea.
00333007 Book/CD Pack.............................. $14.95

8. DISNEY HITS
Beauty and the Beast • Breaking Free • Can You Feel the Love Tonight • Candle on the Water • Colors of the Wind • A Whole New World (Aladdin's Theme) • You'll Be in My Heart • You've Got a Friend in Me.
00333008 Book/CD Pack.............................. $14.95

9. LES MISÉRABLES
At the End of the Day • Bring Him Home • Castle on a Cloud • Do You Hear the People Sing? • Finale • I Dreamed a Dream • On My Own • One Day More.
00333009 Book/CD Pack.............................. $14.99

10. CHRISTMAS FAVORITES
Frosty the Snow Man • The Holiday Season • (There's No Place Like) Home for the Holidays • Little Saint Nick • Merry Christmas, Darling • Santa Claus Is Comin' to Town • Silver Bells • White Christmas.
00333011 Book/CD Pack.............................. $14.95

11. CHRISTMAS TIME IS HERE
Blue Christmas • Christmas Time is Here • Feliz Navidad • Happy Xmas (War Is Over) • I'll Be Home for Christmas • Let It Snow! Let It Snow! Let It Snow! • We Need a Little Christmas • Wonderful Christmastime.
00333012 Book/CD Pack.............................. $14.95

12. THE SOUND OF MUSIC
Climb Ev'ry Mountain • Do-Re-Mi • Edelweiss • The Lonely Goatherd • My Favorite Things • So Long, Farewell • The Sound of Music.
00333019 Book/CD Pack.............................. $14.99

13. CHRISTMAS CAROLS
Angels We Have Heard on High • Deck the Hall • Go, Tell It on the Mountain • Joy to the World • O Come, All Ye Faithful (Adeste Fideles) • O Holy Night • Silent Night • We Wish You a Merry Christmas.
00333020 Book/CD Pack.............................. $14.99

14. GLEE
Can't Fight This Feeling • Don't Stop Believin' • Jump • Keep Holding On • Lean on Me • No Air • Rehab • Somebody to Love.
00333059 Book/CD Pack.............................. $16.99

15. HYMNS
Abide with Me • All Hail the Power of Jesus' Name • Amazing Grace • Be Still My Soul • Blessed Assurance • The Church's One Foundation • Come, Thou Almighty King • It Is Well with My Soul.
00333158 Book/CD Pack.............................. $14.99

16. WORSHIP
All Hail the Power of Jesus' Name • And Can It Be That I Should Gain • Everlasting God • Glory to God Forever • Here I Am to Worship • How Great Is Our God • I Will Rise • A Mighty Fortress Is Our God • My Jesus, I Love Thee • Shout to the Lord • You Are My King (Amazing Love) • Your Name.
00333170 Book/CD Pack.............................. $14.99

17. MORE SONGS FROM GLEE
Empire State of Mind • Firework • Hello, Goodbye • Like a Prayer • Lucky • The Safety Dance • Teenage Dream • To Sir, with Love.
00333377 Book/CD Pack.............................. $17.99

FOR MORE INFORMATION, SEE YOUR LOCAL MUSIC DEALER, OR WRITE TO:

HAL•LEONARD® CORPORATION
7777 W. BLUEMOUND RD. P.O. BOX 13819 MILWAUKEE, WI 53213

Prices, contents, and availability subject to change without notice.

0212